Small Town Boy, Big City Business

A Veteran's Story of Goals, Grit, and Perseverance while Chasing His Passion

Small Town Boy, Big City Business

A VETERAN'S STORY OF GOALS, GRIT, AND PERSEVERANCE WHILE CHASING HIS PASSION

JASON L. RORIE

StoryTerrace

Text Reid Singer, on behalf of StoryTerrace
Design Grade Design and Adeline Media, London
Copyright © Jason L. Rorie

First print June 2020

StoryTerrace

www.StoryTerrace.com

CONTENTS

INTRODUCTION   9

1. GROWING UP   13

2. ENLISTING   25

3. MAKING THE GRADE   41

4. LAUNCHING FROM HOUSTON   53

DEDICATION

This book is dedicated to my family, friends, and colleagues. Without the people who I've met over the years, my decisions would not have been the same. Thank you for helping shape my life. Good and bad. In the end, there is a real benefit to removing the negative from your life and surrounding yourself with awesome people who motivate you and bring out the best in you. Thank you to those people in my life. Also, I appreciate the people who brought negativity into my life; without you, I would not have realized failure and been able to grow from those experiences.

INTRODUCTION

Growing up in the Deep South, I'd seen my fair share of hot summer days. But I caught a glimpse of something entirely different in July 1997, when my rotational crew assumed the watch of the USS Ardent, a small minesweeper off the coast of Bahrain. Outdoor temperatures could climb above 120 degrees when I first arrived in the Persian Gulf, and if I was off duty and permitted to leave the ship, I'd often seek out a cold soda or beer at the Administrative Support Unit (ASU), not far from the pier where we were docked.

The ASU was like a little town. It had a gym, grocery store, barber, and dry cleaner, in addition to a restaurant and bar, and, in the afternoons or evenings, it wasn't unusual to see seasoned officers there mingling with newcomers like myself. At one point, I ended up in conversation with CPO Cramer, the man in charge of communications and information technology for the entire ship.

Sitting at an outdoor picnic table, I remember feeling pretty disarmed. I'd been out of school and part of the rotational crew for five months, and with all my new challenges and responsibilities, I'd grown more confident and independent than I'd ever been as a teenager. Though

SMALL TOWN BOY, BIG CITY BUSINESS

Chief Cramer could be an intimidating guy, and was technically my boss's boss, he wasn't unusually harsh or imperious. I had an awkward moment, however, when he asked me what my goals were for the next four years:

"I wanted to advance from the rank of E1 to E5," I told him. Besides that, I had my sights on the Navy and Marine Corps Achievement Medal, and the Enlisted Surface Warfare Specialist pin. At some point during my time with the crew, I also wanted to be recognized as Sailor of the Quarter.

Chief Cramer looked as if he were suppressing a laugh.

"Ok," he answered. "Let's talk about something more realistic."

Though this reaction caught me off guard, it became a source of motivation over time. Joining the military had been the first truly grown-up decision I ever made. It felt pretty damn good. I was seeking out new opportunities, and willing to take big, calculated risks in order to grow, and, while I knew that all sorts of ups and downs lay in my future, I wasn't particularly frightened or apprehensive. Months earlier, when I signed the final forms to enlist, the recruiter offered some simple instructions: do the best you can, don't half-ass anything, and make sure your ears are open and your mouth is shut. This advice had gotten me through my training and boot camp, and I was convinced it would carry me through my time in the Middle East.

But it ended up carrying me even further. Through the end of my navy service, when I first charted out a civilian career, and up to my present job, managing three thriving businesses, I've found that the world can be awfully generous to people who listen, pay attention, and persevere. By staying true to these simple values, you can accomplish some extraordinary things—my own story is just one example.

Incidentally, I did advance from an E1 to an E5. I also earned the Navy and Marine Corps Achievement Medal, and achieved the Enlisted Surface Warfare Specialist pin, though I never made Sailor of the Quarter (instead, I was named Sailor of the Year in 1999). In a pinch, I can still channel the energy of my younger self, and, with the advantage of experience, I know that his optimism was not misplaced.

I decided to write this book because I believe there might be people out there who've found themselves in a similar situation. I grew up in a working class family, in a tiny rural town, far away from the action of a big city. I never had an inheritance or a trust fund, or any special connections into my profession of choice. But, over the past twenty years, I've learned a thing or two about how ambition plays out in the real world, and about what it really means to chase your passion and persevere. I've also met some pretty cool people and gained some valuable lessons on the road to success. I hope you'll benefit from what I have to share.

1
GROWING UP

Corinth, Mississippi, is about as far as a person could get from the Persian Gulf. When I go there to visit family, leaving behind the traffic and noise of my home near Houston, Texas, I'm often struck by how quiet the neighborhoods still feel, and by how little seems to have changed. Many of the buildings in and around Corinth are cherished relics from the Civil War era, and the area is dotted with old cemeteries and graves of Confederate soldiers—some of whom fought in the Battle of Shiloh, just twenty-five miles away. It's a difficult place to drive through

without feeling a special connection to the past, even if you don't have relatives who can trace your family's history to the early 19th century, when my

SMALL TOWN BOY, BIG CITY BUSINESS

ancestors first settled in the region from Europe. From my research, I've found that the Rories are descendants of the DeGraffenreid family, and that they still have a castle back in Switzerland. While I'd love to visit some day, my roots are here in the United States, and Corinth was my first home.

Unlike the metropolis I live in now, everything in Corinth is within walking distance, and it was easy for me to get around on a bike or on foot. I found kids to play with by wandering to their house and knocking on their door, which is hard to imagine for my own children, who might connect with their friends using an app on their phones. If you ever skipped school, your family would probably find out before you got home,  and parents felt more than comfortable letting their kids wander alone to the nearest playground for a game of pickup baseball. Looking back, I feel grateful to have grown up with so much freedom and space.

My dad left town when I was about a year old, but I was fortunate to have a great mom. Honest, kind, frugal, and hardworking, she set high standards for how I behaved when I was out in the world, and knew how to teach by example. We were far from wealthy, but she never allowed me to feel deprived, and I always had supplies I needed for sports and school. What's more, she wasn't all on her own: I also had two wise and attentive grandparents, whose warm and sheltering home was just a few doors away from ours.

Some of my most vivid memories of early childhood are from their kitchen and their living room, where I watched baseball on TV with my grandfather, who always

sat in his favorite blue chair. Although our region didn't have a home team in the major leagues, there were regular broadcasts of the two nearest franchises, the Chicago Cubs and the Atlanta Braves, and so long as I never blocked my grandfather's view of the screen, I could watch baseball for hours on end. From that cozy space, I developed a passion for the game that has never faded.

To be honest, there was little else that interested me from ages eight to fifteen, apart from the odd game of Mike Tyson's Punch-Out!! or Super Mario Brothers. I was a sought-after pitcher and able to play anywhere on the field the coach

SMALL TOWN BOY, BIG CITY BUSINESS

needed me. And, if I wasn't playing or watching baseball, I was trading cards with other kids at school, seeking out stars of the era like Frank Thomas, Jose Canseco, Mark McGuire, and Barry Bonds. Living in the Southeast, I later became a devoted fan of the Braves and was thrilled to watch Chipper Jones, Greg Maddux, and Steve Avery lead the team to the World Series (durin the nineties, this was practically an annual event).

By the time high school started up, I had trouble finding my niche, so my mom decided to transfer me to a school on the other side of town. Though I didn't realize it at the time, this was actually a huge sacrifice on her part, and just one example of the financial tightrope she had to walk while I was growing up. The new environment allowed me to find some new kids, and I formed close friendships with Jason "Rudy" Randolph, my cousin, Heath Castile, and Richard Russo, his best friend from elementary school. It had only been possible, however, by renting out our house in Corinth. My grades were good, and

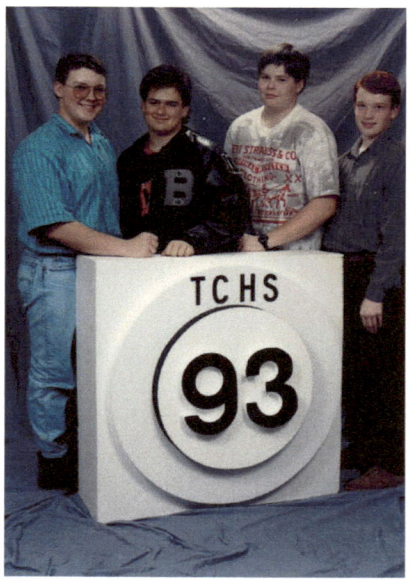

SMALL TOWN BOY, BIG CITY BUSINESS

I'd had a successful season in the new baseball summer league, but if I was going to pay for gas and insurance on the car I drove to school, then I was going to need a part-time job and wouldn't have the time to try out or practice on the varsity team. I hated hanging up my cleats, but the extra cash was important, and, ultimately, this trade-off taught me a valuable lesson about paying my own way. As much fun as I had as a competitive athlete, I think I made the right decision.

What's more, I was developing new interests and hobbies that would turn out to be just as rewarding as baseball. In the summer of 1995, my mother brought home a Packard Bell computer from the local Walmart. We installed a 28800 baud rate external dial-up modem—considered blazingly fast at the time—and, though the system didn't look like much, it easily surpassed the family Nintendo as the most sophisticated machine in our home. Laptops were far from universal in those days, and mobile tablets were still a long way off, but many people could afford desktop models like the one my mother bought, which, for all their limitations, could do some remarkable things. Through this mysterious grey box sitting on our desk, I felt as though I could access a fascinating new world.

The more I read, the more I wanted to know about how computers work, how they're built, and how they can be repaired or improved. Every now and then, I'd have the money for an upgraded component, which a friend of a friend

SMALL TOWN BOY, BIG CITY BUSINESS

TCHS Word Processing Students Spread Good Will Abroad

could install by hand, and I'd watch enthusiastically as they cracked open the machine to reveal its inner circuitry. In school, I'd always been a decent student, but preferred to fly under the radar, and never tried to push myself with higher-level classes in physics or calculus. By comparison, everything I learned in this new field was voluntary. And, because I was enjoying myself while quickly picking up the knowledge, it never felt like work.

I'm not sure when it occurred to me that computers could be more than a hobby. This changed dramatically, however, during the fall of our senior year, when my friend Rudy leaned towards my desk during English class and asked me a question that would change the course of my life.

"I'm thinking about joining the military," he said. "Do you want to go with me?"

The armed services had a mixed appeal for me at first. Enlisting was the kind of thing you'd expect from my late grandfather—who, before he worked at a Dr. Pepper bottling plant, had been part of an infantry unit that landed in

SMALL TOWN BOY, BIG CITY BUSINESS

Normandy on D-Day. He actually spent six months in a German POW camp, and was awarded a Purple Heart, before being discharged. But he hadn't made a career out of the Army, and, while I'm sure he would have been pleased that I was following a similar path, it wasn't something we'd talked about much when  I was growing up. Here and there, I'd also met veterans who said they joined the service to avoid jail time—an old-fashioned remedy for petty crime, no longer in practice, and which didn't really apply to my situation. Besides this, I've met folks who were inspired by a school field trip to a museum ship like the USS Texas, near Houston, which enlivened their connections to the military and its history.

This is much easier for me to sympathize with, though I also had some reasons for joining that were more practical. When many of our classmates were taking the SATs, or sending off their applications to college, there were plenty of kids who, like me, needed to get a job and find some financial security first. In theory, by joining the service, I could make enough money to earn my degree later on, and acquire all sorts of valuable skills. I could choose my own specialty and have a head start when I entered the civilian workforce.

For his part, Rudy was drawn to the physical and personal development aspects of the military. Between our sophomore and junior year, he'd made a small project out of losing weight, and, by following a strict diet and exercise plan, he'd gotten into phenomenal shape. When we were considering which branch to join, Rudy had wondered out loud if he could survive the famously grueling tests and training required for joining the Navy SEALs.

My own motivations had less to do with parachute school and more to do with learning about computers. In fact, one of the biggest reasons we chose the navy over other branches was because the recruiter lived a little closer to us, which meant we could talk a little bit more about technical and career training. A recruiter's job, after all, is to recruit, and they'll devote all sorts of attention and resources to making their branch look as attractive as possible, answering every last question from their potential applicants. I took what I heard with a grain of salt and tried not to be taken in by what was effectively a salesman's pitch about exciting work, great pay, and travel to exotic places. The basics, however, sounded pretty good to me: I wouldn't be firing any cannons or jumping out of any planes, but I'd be working hard for a steady paycheck, and acquiring real-world skills that would be attractive to future employers.

SMALL TOWN BOY, BIG CITY BUSINESS

Later that fall, Rudy and I began filling out the initial paperwork and then travelled two hours to Memphis for the physical exam. In February 1996, we signed the final documents for a delayed entry program and swore ourselves in, with a commitment to leave for boot camp the following August. Rudy and I finished the last semester, graduated in good standing, and, for the next several months, our plans seemed set in stone.

Then, one day, they weren't. After the tragic passing of a close friend, Rudy was having a difficult time. He'd started to think about everything he would leave behind in Iuka, the town near Corinth where he lived, and all the friends and relatives he wouldn't be able to see while we were away. It wasn't hard for me to sympathize—besides my mother, grandparents, and friends, I'd grown close with Kacey and Lacey, twin half-sisters from my dad's second marriage, and their mother, Debbie, all of whom now lived nearby. Just over a month before it was time to ship off, Rudy called to let me know he wasn't going, which put me in a difficult position. I wasn't

SMALL TOWN BOY, BIG CITY BUSINESS

sure if I could go without my best friend, and so I promptly followed suit and told my family and the recruiter that I'd be staying home.

At first, it looked as if I would simply get a job at a local factory, which produced particle board panels for inexpensive, ready-to-assemble furniture. From what I could tell, there weren't many other opportunities for someone with only a high school diploma, and I felt anxious, as if I was in some sort of limbo. It was a tough environment, especially during the height of the summer, since the building had no air conditioning. When I'd been there for a couple of weeks, some of the older, middle-aged guys around my work station started to talk about the realities of life in the factory, and the toll it had taken on their bodies. Many talked about the boredom of their jobs, or the physical breakdown they'd experienced over the decades. A few of them flatly told me to find something else to do with my life.

If I had any other way of making a living, they said, then this probably wasn't my kind of place. Eventually, something in me clicked. Corinth was a wonderful town, but if I wanted to open up doors, and make something of myself, then I couldn't stick around. That evening, I came home after work and had a heart-to-heart talk with my mom.

I told her I was thinking of leaving after all and going to boot camp, even if it was by myself. I wanted to know

SMALL TOWN BOY, BIG CITY BUSINESS

what she thought about me entering the navy alone, and I was relieved to hear that she would have my back, no matter what I decided to do. With her support, I felt comfortable telling everyone else that I was sticking to the original plan, including Debbie and my half-sisters, who I joined for a short vacation in St. Louis, Missouri, so that we could say our goodbyes. The funniest reaction probably came when I called the recruiting office to tell them I was going after all.

"Yeah," they answered, "that's what we figured you'd do."

I was due at boot camp a few weeks later, on August 20, 1996. After a 90-minute flight from Memphis International Airport, and a 30-mile bus ride from Chicago, I would arrive in Naval Station Great Lakes, near the Wisconsin border, where Lake Michigan was visible from the window of my barrack. It was the furthest north that I'd ever been.

There was no point in maintaining the rosy picture of what I was actually getting into, and I gave no further thought to the rainbows and unicorns of the recruiters' pitch. Instead, I tried to remember their last bit of advice:

keep your ears open and your mouth shut, don't half-ass anything, and do what you're asked. It sounded simple enough, though I had no idea how powerful these words would actually be.

2

ENLISTING

When I stepped onto the bus at O'Hare International Airport and found my seat, I thought about how much it differed from the comfortable ride I'd taken months earlier to get my physical in Memphis. The recruiter had actually taken the time to drive me and Rudy himself, in a government car, though I realized this was probably just a part of the salesman's treatment, and only lasted as long as I could still back out. As I stared out the window of that Greyhound, the phrase, "no service after sale," was ringing in my head. Now that they had me, they had me.

Shortly after arriving at Great Lakes, I had another physical and was fitted for a new set of clothes. We were then introduced to our recruit division commanders (RDC): Chief Williams, Petty Officer Corbin, and Petty Officer Petermore, who gave instructions for how we should store our gear, fold our pants and shirts, and keep our bunk tidy. The next few weeks were a torrent of classes, marches, lectures, and

physical training, some of which could be pretty tough, but, compared to other boot camp experiences I'd heard about, our RDCs were pretty easygoing.

This was simply the luck of the draw. Later on, I was exposed to an RDC who shouted in the scratchy voice of a heavy smoker, stood at five-feet-four-inches with his boots on, and wore aviators no matter the time of day (though formally known as Petty Officer Lasley, many recruits referred to him as Sergeant Slaughter). The people in charge of the female's divisions were reputed to be tougher than the men's, and I'm sure that there were others who were even scarier. Years later, I would talk to fellow veterans for whom boot camp had been a non-stop blur of running, calisthenics, and drills. I honestly don't know if we ended up with a lazier crew, but this wasn't how things turned out for our division. My biggest burden was sleep deprivation, and, after a while, I could even grow accustomed to starting my day at four o'clock in the morning, when the wind coming off the lake was at its coldest.

SMALL TOWN BOY, BIG CITY BUSINESS

Over the next eight weeks, our group was put through confidence courses and fire safety drills. We swam laps in the pool, studied the laws of armed conflict, and rehearsed emergency situations on a simulator training ship. There was instruction in nomenclature and sea craft identification, and I learned quite a bit about riflery, basic seamanship, and first aid. Eventually, we were also introduced to the navy's shipboard communication gear. By the fourth or fifth week, I got to learn more about my intended specialty and talk to people with more experience about what my post-graduation job training would be like.

After Pass-In-Review, the military's term for boot camp graduation, we were formally inducted into the service. The next step was to register for US Navy A School, where we'd receive specific training for our intended specialty. The base where A School took place was literally across the street from where we'd gone to boot camp, and it covered all the technical knowledge I would need to be a radioman—a rating for communications specialists, now referred to as information systems technicians. Depending on the rating, the length of an A School course can last from less than a month to over a year, but I ultimately stayed for sixteen weeks.

SMALL TOWN BOY, BIG CITY BUSINESS

A School was a little bit less intense than boot camp and a little more like twelfth grade. I got to socialize a little bit more, and I became friends with fellow radiomen-in-training from all over the country, including an Arkansan named Roger Eades and northerners like Daniel Mahaven and Michael Aquilino. Though I was certain that my own Southern accent had faded, and even struggled now to understand my relatives when I called them in Mississippi, my regional dialect became an object of fascination (and some teasing) from my classmates, who'd grown up in Pittsburgh or New Jersey. We got along well, however, and when we were permitted to leave the vicinity of the base, we'd have fun by renting out a hotel room in town or by traveling to Chicago to hang out or grab dinner.

Mostly, though, we were studying. For the rest of the fall, and right up until Christmas of 1996, I was steadily introduced to use teletypes and receivers, learned to read call signs, and acquainted myself with the unique hybrid of computers and analog radio equipment used on ships and submarines. Before school was over, we were expected

SMALL TOWN BOY, BIG CITY BUSINESS

to master a wide array of different communications systems, involving complex satellite technology, microwave signals, and simple two-way radios. The most efficient way for crews to stay in touch can depend on whether they're docked or at sea, within each other's line of sight, or thousands of miles apart, and a competent radioman needed to know which patch cable to connect with which medium. The navy was embracing digital technology at a gradual pace, and if my active duty assignment was on a ship with old school circuitry, then I needed to be ready for that as well.

On top of all of this, the message traffic I'd be responsible for was often classified and could only be read using special decryption devices. Using these devices would be an essential part of my job, and so I would need a security clearance in order to qualify, which meant that while the rest of my training was taking place, the Department of the Navy was conducting a background check. Though I didn't find out about it until a few months later, some folks went so far as to visit my hometown, where they verified basic facts about my family and education, and even talked to my neighbors about what I was like. They did a thorough job, but I was never interrogated, or asked to do anything more arduous than fill out a form. Down the road, when I'd bought a house and registered my first business, I found this vetting process was headache-free by comparison.

A few students I met in A School mentioned that if we placed at the top of our class, we might have some say in

SMALL TOWN BOY, BIG CITY BUSINESS

where we ended up serving, and could potentially pick our duty station. This may have been just a rumor. I graduated in March 1997 and was assigned to Mine Countermeasures Rotational Crew Bravo, stationed at Naval Station Ingleside, Texas, near Corpus Christi. I was informed shortly afterwards that I'd be leaving for the Middle East the following summer, and, in June, I packed my bags and traveled to the Persian Gulf.

My new home was the ASU, or Administrative Support Unit, now known as Naval Support Activity Bahrain, outside the capital city of Manama, and my work would be on the USS Ardent. With only 84 men and women on board at any time, our crew was tiny when compared to other vessels, and, though it didn't have the prestige of a famous aircraft carrier or nuclear submarine, I quickly came to appreciate the advantages of a smaller team. While larger ships might spend weeks or months without seeing land, our food storage was limited, so we were never expected to stay at sea for very long. It took time for me to get accustomed to

sleeping on coffin racks, and some of the taller guys probably felt pretty cramped, but I always had a few inches to move around.

More important than that, of course, were the

SMALL TOWN BOY, BIG CITY BUSINESS

relationships you tend to build in such close quarters. I was working, eating, and spending my free time with the same people every day. We came to lean on each other, sometimes literally, and, in the long run, these circumstances led to a greater feeling of affinity and trust. Furthermore, because I never forgot the recruiter's advice to always listen and do my best, I found myself taking on more sophisticated tasks and bigger responsibilities that wouldn't have been possible for younger or lower-ranking sailors on bigger vessels. The navy had promised a challenging, hands-on learning experience, and, so far, it had delivered.

My job as a radioman was pretty straightforward. I didn't get to install or perform repairs on the ship's hardware, but this was probably just as well since the equipment was almost entirely analog and some parts relied on World War II technology. Messages were sent electronically, in a slightly simplified form of email, and I was a kind of processor, monitoring the tractor-feed pages that were printed out near my work station. Most of what I read was generic information, but we had to be on alert in case an important memo came in from an admiral stationed on shore, and if something more sensitive came through, I'd have to know who to contact first. The work could be tedious at times but not nearly as bad as other navy jobs, such as painting the ship or working in the engine room. The more I learned the craft of the job, the more grateful I felt for my assignment.

SMALL TOWN BOY, BIG CITY BUSINESS

On a typical day, I'd wake up at six o'clock, grab a quick breakfast, and head to my work area. At seven, there was a brief staff meeting called a muster, where the department heads  would make sure no one was missing, and hand out the day's to-do lists. Since we weren't at war, an immense amount of time was devoted to safety and role-playing drills, designed to simulate the feeling of a real emergency. Just as a car can't stay stationary for months on end without sacrificing performance, a ship and its crew must always be at least moderately active in order to keep their edge. In some scenarios, we were told about an imaginary fire on the ship, which we'd have to contain and extinguish, or an imaginary water-based mine, which we'd have to defuse or detonate before it could harm other ships. Other times, we were told there was a chemical attack, ship to flooding, or that we needed to access low-running supplies from another vessel.

Every now and then, an inspector would be on board to watch our response, ask us questions, and give us a grade for readiness and competency. If there was a fire, they asked, where would our oxygen masks be? How would we know when the flames were under control? These rapid fire quizzes could be particularly nerve-wracking during a fire

SMALL TOWN BOY, BIG CITY BUSINESS

drill in the main space, where the engines were housed, and where I was sometimes part of the firefighting team. The role had nothing to do with communications, of course, and I wouldn't have had such an opportunity on a bigger ship, but, on the USS Ardent, I got to see firsthand how the fire was handled.

If it got worse, I got to see how we would abandon ship. While one group might be tasked with finding and deploying lifeboats, the communications department was often responsible for destroying codebooks and decryption equipment, which contained classified material that couldn't be leaked (the routine could involve putting printed pages into a special envelope and burning it, or dropping the equipment into a bag and throwing it overboard, along with a hunk of concrete to ensure that it would sink). Drills could be an intense experience, sometimes lasting over four hours, and the bigger the exercise the more parts of the ship were involved. It was fascinating to see how we all came together under pressure. Whether you were on the deck department, ensuring that the ship and anchors were clean, or on the weapons department in charge of the vessel's firepower,

SMALL TOWN BOY, BIG CITY BUSINESS

everyone had an important role to play, and everyone had to be connected.

After a full day of managing the crew's communications, we'd have some time to read, listen to music, and socialize before supper. Hours were somewhat shorter when the ship was docked, so I'd often join other radiomen in the ASU's recreation area, where you could watch movies or play pool. On occasion, we had the opportunity to explore the town of

Manama. Our officers knew that this was the first time that many of us had ever visited a foreign country, and they had strict instructions for how we behaved among the general public.

The people I met in the Middle East were warm and cordial and not at all hostile to Americans. Although, there were facts about their culture that we could not allow to slip. Certain gestures, which we'd always thought of as friendly, could be deeply offensive to people living in the Persian Gulf; even something as simple as a thumbs up could be taken for flashing your middle finger. If we visited a hookah bar, and smoked a flavored tobacco called shisha while sitting on the floor, then we had to be careful not to show the soles of our shoes, which is a grave insult in that part of the world. I was

SMALL TOWN BOY, BIG CITY BUSINESS

particularly surprised by some of the rules governing inland travel for sailors, like myself, who occasionally had to drive a car from base to base on an international license: if I hit a poor person, the locals told me, it would be a serious matter. But not as serious as hitting a camel.

Beyond cultural sensitivity, there were also safety and intelligence issues for us to keep in mind. Every sailor traveling off-base had to observe a buddy system, and we were advised against following any kind of routine that other people could learn to observe and predict. Whereas an infraction like fighting could be dealt with harshly if it took place on board the ship, the consequences could be even more serious if it took place among the civilian population, and we were told to avoid it at all costs. Certain topics of conversation, such as the position of other vessels, was considered off-limits when we were in public, since the information was often classified, though many people in Manama could do their own fact-finding without our help. Several days before an aircraft carrier came to port, I would notice that the city's cab drivers had tripled their rates. Clearly, the folks who lived in Bahrain knew more than they always let on.

Back on the ship, I continued to work hard at my job, hoping to earn the admiration of people like Chief Cramer, who ran the communications department. On a ship like ours, a chief petty officer is a little like a general manager who works with other general managers on the ship, or at

SMALL TOWN BOY, BIG CITY BUSINESS

shore, to make big-picture decisions about the future of the vessel. It's a position you could only reach after many years of service, and, given how important rank was to every relationship and social interaction in the navy, Chief Cramer enjoyed a special level of authority and respect. At the same time, he wasn't unusually big or aggressive and didn't manifest the traits of a stereotypical navy boss—besides the obligatory moustache. It might have been because he was such a nice guy that I felt so comfortable when we finally sat side by side on that picnic table at the base, and he asked me what my goals were.

I don't know what I expected when I told him about earning the Enlisted Surface Warfare Specialist pin, or getting recognized as Sailor of the Quarter. By adolescent standards, I was a pretty humble kid and didn't think he'd respond by patting me on the back, or  congratulating me for my competitive spirit. On the other hand, wasn't it part of his job to lift up and inspire the next generation of sailors? Or to at least encourage the ones who were ready and driven?

SMALL TOWN BOY, BIG CITY BUSINESS

I'm sure his intentions were good, but I was surprised to hear him say that those were lofty goals, and that I might not want to set my hopes quite so high. And, while I didn't bear Chief Cramer any ill-will, a big part of me wanted to prove him wrong. Halfway through my term, I'd already advanced from an E1 to an E3 and was actively chasing the other qualifications—including the Enlisted Surface Warfare Specialist (ESWS) pin.

ESWS is a title of expertise, which sailors often display besides their name, like DDS or PhD. In order to earn the pin, I needed to talk to men all over the ship and avail myself to whatever tests of knowledge they felt like throwing my way. If I could prove I knew the basics of the ship's defense mechanisms, combat systems, damage control, or force protection, then they would sign their name to my examination book. Once I'd collected every signature, I applied to take the oral exam, where I would answer question after question from senior officers and chiefs with decades of experience. I still remember how it felt to stand in the ship's chief's

SMALL TOWN BOY, BIG CITY BUSINESS

mess while they listened to me speak, or to wait nervously outside while they assessed my performance in private. When the officers finally invited me back inside, and told me I'd passed, it was one of the proudest moments of my time in the navy.

In my first four years, I spent two periods of six months in the Middle East. The remainder of my term was spent at the base in Ingleside, Texas, which was obviously a more familiar environment. Though I didn't have a lot of vacation time to visit my family, I felt at home in the nearby city of Corpus Christi, and I got to know the area well. I had my own apartment, and enjoyed living in such a sunny, low-key town with a tight group of friends from work. Even after hours, we did just about everything together; throwing a

frisbee around at the beach, sipping beers at the bars or restaurants downtown, or just hanging out at each other's apartments where we'd gripe about our jobs, or have age-appropriate debates about cars and girls. In many ways, these were some of the happiest times of my life. I'm still close with Gary Moore, who still lives in the Corpus area, and Jake Sims and Roger Eades, who both live in the Houston area.

SMALL TOWN BOY, BIG CITY BUSINESS

Living in Corpus was a great experience, but, in early 2000, it was time for me to make another big decision. My four-year stint in the navy was coming to an end, and I'd fallen in love with South Texas. I told the detailer, a job negotiator for the Navy, that I was willing to reenlist, provided I could keep working at a base nearby. One option was to stay in the region and agree to another, six-year term, though this felt like an awfully big time commitment. Or, I could have agreed to a second four-year term, but I would have to go overseas. Looking back, it's occurred to me that if I'd taken this route then I could have potentially lived in a much more comfortable base in a country like Italy, but, at the time, this wasn't especially enticing. After a month or so of negotiation, the recruiter and I still couldn't work out a deal, and so I prepared to leave the service the following summer.

My timing wasn't half bad. I reconnected with my old pal Rudy, who ended up serving for six years in the Army National Guard, and we  got to talking about our options and ways of finding work. Rudy's father was employed with Corbin Communications, a company based in Plano, Texas, who needed someone on hand in the northern Alabama region. On the strength of our friendship, and my status as a veteran, the folks at

SMALL TOWN BOY, BIG CITY BUSINESS

Corbin suggested I could work with them. I decided that Huntsville, a city just two hours away from my mom's house in Corinth, would be an ideal place for me to go back to school and formalize my education in IT.

This, again, was just the kind of outcome the Navy had promised when I was a high school senior. I was grateful for their help and for everything the service had taught me, but the time felt right to try and challenge myself in a new way. In August, I packed up everything in my Corpus apartment and prepared to move back east.

3

MAKING THE GRADE

Few cities in America have done more for engineers, programmers, and developers than Huntsville. Ever since the Cold War, when the Marshall Space Flight Center was constructed in town, Rocket City has enjoyed a special relationship with NASA and the Department of Defense, and, over the decades, it's become a uniquely welcoming place for people who like to build and work on machines. Northern Alabama is still one of the most  robust tech hubs in the country and was a perfect fit for a young person starting out in the profession while trying to find his niche. In the late summer of 2000, the region had so many satellite towers that my supervisors at Corbin Communications didn't really care where I lived, so long as it was somewhere in-state.

SMALL TOWN BOY, BIG CITY BUSINESS

My first few months in Huntsville, however, were pretty tough. I had no trouble moving into an apartment, and the supervisor who drove from Memphis to conduct my orientation was helpful and polite, but, once he was finished, I was on my own. Culture shock is no joke. It was difficult meeting new people, and, after four years of always being around other sailors, some of whom were still my closest friends, I had trouble adjusting and developing a new routine. Staying in touch with everyone I missed back in Corpus, and talking to them on the phone as frequently as I did, I felt some temptation to change course yet again and reenlist. Recruiters told me that for 90 days after I was discharged, it would be possible to go right back into service, complete with the same job and rank, as if you'd never left. For a short time, this sounded appealing but the more I thought about it, the more I worried about missing out on college.

Ultimately, I decided to suck it up and give civilian life a try. I settled into my new position as a field technician for Corbin, and, a few months later, I enrolled in night classes in the computer science program at Calhoun Community College where I could potentially earn an associate's degree. Though I enjoyed the course in HTML, the code used for building web sites, topics like programming and software left me feeling uninspired, so I considered transferring to Virginia College, a vocational school, where 90 percent of the curriculum would focus on IT.

SMALL TOWN BOY, BIG CITY BUSINESS

When I talked to an enrollment counselor, she started telling me about the benefits made available through the Department of Veterans Affairs (VA). If I were to stay on a web design path, I could take a one-year certificate program, though this is not exactly the same as a degree, and the VA wouldn't pay my tuition. The VA would, however, cover a two-year associate's degree in network engineering, which caught my attention, and so I picked up a flier about the program and started to read. The course descriptions looked intense and were full of references to companies like Microsoft, Cisco and CompTIA.

"This is high-level engineering," I thought. "It looks really difficult."

It wasn't hard to imagine getting overwhelmed. At the time, I understood the basics of how computers operated, but I knew very little about building networks or servers. On the other hand, getting the VA to pay for my education sounded like a pretty sweet deal. Not long after leaving the counselor's office, I filled out the paperwork to register.

Starting in March 2002, I began the introductory course in the communications standards that computers use to talk to each other. Because I was already familiar with hardware components and how they were repaired, I could gain some initial credit just by reading a book on the A+ (A Plus), an entry-level certification for system installation and maintenance, and taking the test. This set me six months ahead of the two-year program, but other subjects were much less familiar and were taught at a much faster pace. Finding time to read and study at home was a challenge in itself, since I was still at work for at least eight hours a day.

Things got even more complicated when financial issues forced Corbin into a round of lay-offs. I'd barely gotten on my feet in my new home, but now I was suddenly out of a

job, and so I needed to do some serious improvising if I was going to stay in school. After sending out copies of my resume to everyone in town, I found work doing basic computer repairs for a mom and pop shop. Later on, I fell into a warehouse position at Gateway, a company that was riding high at the time and had their own retail branches. My days could be exhaustingly long, but I was enjoying school more than I ever had, and, though I was under a lot of stress, I tended to embrace the difficulties more than I resented them.

When the going gets tough, you're likely to fall back into your old habits. My own habits were ingrained in the Navy, which put me at a huge advantage. When I learned that an award was given to the top-performing student in every class, I made it my goal to win it and spent every

SMALL TOWN BOY, BIG CITY BUSINESS

extra hour I could studying or in the lab. Even if we were asked to digest a 900-page textbook in a few weeks, I read every chapter twice and tried to absorb every word. My own program was particularly demanding, and the dropout rate was ridiculously high: out of 28 people in the program with me, only three of us lasted to the end, but instructors like Jessie Weems, now a great friend, made the school not so stressful.

After eighteen months, I graduated with ten or twelve new certifications, and the academic achievement award for all six of my classes. From there, I was able to land a consulting job and get my first taste of the business-to-business style that I'd pursue with my own companies. I got a lot of satisfaction from driving around and dealing with different issues at different organizations, but I was frustrated with the pay, which was about half the hourly rate of someone with a four-year degree. I had a respectable skill set, and was good at my job, but it was clear that I needed more formal education, and so I enrolled in a bachelor's degree in technology management at Athens State University, about forty minutes west of Huntsville.

SMALL TOWN BOY, BIG CITY BUSINESS

Over the next two years, I picked up a few more certifications and held a handful of IT positions where I'd build or maintain networks and servers around the state. Some of my arrangements with employers were pretty lean, and, for a while, I was only paid for the billable hours I spent in a client's office, with no benefits. Over time, I had to learn not only to be a consultant and an engineer, but a marketing rep, an accountant, a salesman, and an office administrator. While working for a company called Techni-core, I was expected to do more or less everything but my own bookkeeping. There were times when I felt overworked, but I learned a lot from having all these extra responsibilities. In 2005, I was offered a full-time position, with benefits, at a thriving multinational called Aviagen, which specialized in breeding and product development for the poultry industry. I stayed there for a year, keeping the company's IT infrastructure running smoothly and felt proud of how much I'd accomplished.

Clearly, I was making progress, but I still didn't feel grounded, and I sorely missed living in Texas. When I dropped into the old stomping ground for a wedding, and spent three days laughing and reminiscing with guys I'd known since my early twenties, it dawned on me that for all that Huntsville offered, it wasn't where I felt at home.

When I went back to Alabama, and called up my old friends or navy buddies, they asked me when I was moving back. I didn't have an answer for them until mid-2006,

SMALL TOWN BOY, BIG CITY BUSINESS

when an old colleague reached out and told me about Spring Medical Systems, a company based out of Houston, where he was vice president. Their focus was software, but many of their clients were having problems that could be better addressed by a networking expert. It sounded like a potential match, and so I flew over from Huntsville for an interview.

What followed was probably the easiest hiring process I'd ever been through. I had my meeting in Houston on a Saturday, returned home on Sunday, and was offered a job the following Monday. Though I would have to accept a pay cut, and move to a city with a higher cost of living, my new employers gave me every assurance that I would have the time and space to start my own network consulting business, using the skills I'd learned as a by-the-hour employee to carve out a niche in the market. As well as I can remember, one of my first clients had been a manufacturer that built refrigeration and cooling systems for the food and agricultural sector. They were happy with the work I did and referred me to their friends.

By the end of the year, I was once again living in a new city, just a few hours from Corpus, and working at one of the most robust tech companies in the region. In 2006, Spring Medical was named in the Houston Business Journal's Fast Tech 50, and the entire staff got to attend an awards luncheon at a hotel downtown, where I watched as one executive after another was invited up onto the stage. As our own company president accepted the award and had his picture taken, I thought about how cool it would be to have my own consulting business honored in the same way. Now that I was back in the Lone Star State, it felt like the sky was the limit.

In the same way that a realtor looks to sell bigger and more elaborate homes, I was hungry to challenge myself by working on bigger and more complex servers. Each new account felt like a new puzzle, whether it was an insurance agency, an accounting firm, a manufacturing client, or a company that builds playgrounds. By moving from problem to problem, day after day, I could constantly test my mind and everything I'd learned, just as the crew of a minesweeper can do a transport drill on one day, or a fire drill on another. Solving these puzzles often took time, and I could be humbled very quickly, but no two days were the same, and the sheer variety of businesses for me to work with was a big part of the fun.

I also got a lot out of helping people. From my experience at companies like Techni-core in Huntsville, and from working as my own boss in Houston, I came to realize that no matter where I was living, small business owners would

SMALL TOWN BOY, BIG CITY BUSINESS

have a lot of the same priorities and concerns. A long time ago, these guys and girls had taken an inventory of their talents, adapted those talents to the needs of the market, and figured out a way to build value. Now that they were on their feet, they wanted an operation that would be productive, efficient, competitive, and secure, while providing the best possible service to their customers.

In other words, they were a lot like me. Their decision to outsource their IT needs to a small company like mine, rather than hiring a full-time employee, was borne out of necessity and thrift. I could identify with who they were and what they were trying to do, which meant that I could listen with a heightened level of empathy and respect when they talked about the unique challenges of their organization.

Once again, my navy recruiter's advice was coming in handy. Simply by doing my best, keeping my ears open, and my mouth shut, I could pick things up quickly and adapt to any situation. This made me valuable to the folks I knew at Spring Medical and my next day job at Petroleum Geo-Services, a multinational that provides seismic data and imaging to the oil and gas industry.

Naturally, it also helped me in my own venture, where competence and technical knowledge on their own were not a guarantee of success. To really thrive, I'd need to build a reputation through word-of-mouth recommendations. People would figure out that I was an honest and responsive operator but only after I'd spent many years returning calls and emails, listening to clients, and sorting out any problem they threw my way. To this day, I hang my hat on the company's ability to respond to every call or email within thirty minutes or less, whether it's from a prospective customer or someone who already knows us well. By meeting this standard, we could distinguish ourselves from the competition, who might take two or three days to answer their messages.

Looking back, I've come to appreciate why the first two years of a new venture can be so trying, and why it's so important to have an effective strategy for marketing and sales. Even if I was the greatest engineer in the world, capable of helping people in all sorts of ways, I would only ever find new accounts and grow the business if I could form useful contacts and promote my services.

With this in mind, I talked to Larry Lipton, an associate of my Navy buddy, Gary Moore's father, who suggested I try connecting with other businesses through the local Chamber of Commerce. As time went on, I started attending more conferences and events and exchanging advice with my peers. At every opportunity I had, I talked about my own company, first called Superior IT Solutions, which we later changed to Elevated Technologies. If people were curious about what we did, I'd tell them a little bit more about my background and specialties and ask if they had any computer or server issues that needed to be addressed.

Once you're on a roll, it can be hard to get out of selling mode. At a certain point, I couldn't even go to a doctor's appointment without posing a few questions about his office IT infrastructure, how it was set up, and whether there was anything I could do for them. There were no guarantees that my company would succeed, and there were many months in which my self-employment income oscillated between nothing and next-to-nothing. But I was passionate about what I was doing, and I held fast to my vision of the future.

4

LAUNCHING FROM HOUSTON

After I'd been living in Houston for about two-and-a-half years, Elevated Technologies began to find its stride. My service was as fast, thoughtful, and attentive as I could make it, and I was introducing myself wherever I could, filling my schedule with networking breakfasts, and face-to-face meetings with potential leads. As I started attracting bigger accounts, I switched from a by-the-hour model to a by-the-month arrangement, which generated  more revenue, and expanded my profit margins. Finally, in the fall of 2008, my workload and income reached a tipping point, and I handed in my notice to Petroleum Geo-Services. By the end of the year, I was working for myself full-time.

SMALL TOWN BOY, BIG CITY BUSINESS

This was a new world for me, demanding a radically new skill set. Since I had no budget for an accountant, I downloaded a copy of Quickbooks, and my friends were soon laughing at the intricately dorky spreadsheets I used to calculate my profits. Similarly, it would be years before I could buy print ads and mail out letters and postcards to promote the company, and so I found less expensive ways to get the word out and became adept at talking up my skills in person. Without quite expecting it, I began to take on responsibilities that had nothing to do with building an office network, or fixing a server, and uncovered some talents I didn't appreciate before.

Sales, for example, was not something I'd ever really thought about for the first half of my life, but it didn't take long for me to start noticing the hit of adrenaline that comes with closing a deal. Once I felt that rush, I wanted to chase it again and again; if I walked out of a meeting, checked my email, and found a message from someone interested in switching IT companies, I'd smile like a kid in a candy store. It sounds like a cliché, but if you enjoy what you do then you'll never work a day in your life. Putting the work in with my clients was time-consuming, and rarely glamorous, but I was having a ball, especially once those positive referrals started to accumulate.

Making sales was a new thing for me and so was being an executive. Teamwork and group cohesion had been a big part of my life in the Navy, but I never reached a high enough rank to actually be in charge of a large group, and I had no formal education in management. For the first several years of its existence, Elevated Technologies had been a one-man band, and there was a certain comfort in doing every job myself, and in having complete control over how the work was done. At the same time, my choice to operate alone put a necessary cap on the number of clients I could effectively serve. While this might not have been a problem if I was working in a small town with few competitors, I was now living in a massive city, and sharing space with tech giants and competitors that were much larger than me. If I wanted to make my business grow, I'd have to delegate tasks to people I'd selected and trained, and who I was confident would do as thorough a job as I did.

The hiring process was yet another patch of unfamiliar territory, but I made some decent choices and was fortunate to find people I could rely on. These days, I rarely provide direct service myself, and some of my employees have rightfully teased me for getting rusty, but I used to have a lot more dirt under my fingernails. When my own team members saw the hours I put in, the attention to detail I tried to sustain, and the passion I had for helping our customers, it set the pace for the rest of the team and established a working style that they'd emulate when I wasn't around.

Leadership-by-example is a powerful thing, but so is trial-and-error, and, to be frank, the core of my management style was formed by making rookie mistakes.

SMALL TOWN BOY, BIG CITY BUSINESS

It was only after making my first hires, for example, that I realized how difficult it can be to keep track of employees' work, and why things like checklists could be so valuable for holding them accountable and for keeping our service uniform and consistent. I tried to keep an eye on tension between colleagues, which could affect productivity, but there were times when I was too busy or preoccupied to notice it, and so I came to rely on the sharp eyes of my co-managers, including Austin Elwell, who I brought on in 2010. The more I opened myself up to the expertise of people like Austin, the easier it was to break through certain plateaus in the company's performance and get the most out of my staff.

As I gained professional experience, both as an engineer and as an entrepreneur, I started to meet more people who are starting out and eager for some words of wisdom. I've gotten to know the field pretty well, but there really isn't a magic wand or secret weapon I can point to—besides the principles I'd been practicing since I got out of high school.

SMALL TOWN BOY, BIG CITY BUSINESS

Much of this goes back to what I learned from my mother, who didn't always enjoy her wor, and who told me as I got older to make sure I found an occupation that was truly fulfilling.

Without a passion for the work, and a willingness to persevere, I'm sure I would have run out of steam a long time ago. This, essentially, is the most important lesson from my years of experience, and it applies no matter what profession you're in: if you truly care, and you feel a genuine stake in your clients' businesses, then you'll find the strength to keep grinding, even when things get difficult.

For folks in the IT space, my best advice has had to do with ethics. If a client is paying you money to work on their computers, it's probably because they don't quite understand how they work, and don't have the time or ability to learn. They're willing to put some basic faith in you, and your expertise, and they believe that you'll identify their problems accurately, explain them in plain English, and sort them out without disturbing the rhythm of their organization.

I know that it's on me to honor these expectations. Like home contracting or auto repair, the IT and computing fields have been disproportionately affected by folks who are willing to abuse or overstate their knowledge. When you're working with highly sophisticated machines, there can be all sorts of opportunities to exaggerate their complexity, or take

SMALL TOWN BOY, BIG CITY BUSINESS

unnecessary extra time with repairs. In this environment, it's been absolutely imperative for me to deal with my clients plainly and to always be truthful about what they really need. Honesty is the best policy, and, in the long run, it's been good for business.

This point is especially salient when it comes to protection and security. In the times we're living in, every enterprise under the sun is relying on digital technology to keep afloat, and the pressure has never been greater on engineers to keep networks defended from intrusion. Many network consultants simply don't understand this aspect of the profession, or have become complacent with a "good enough" approach, and don't realize their mistake until they've lost their client's data. If you can't deliver on your promises, or if a client feels like they can't trust you, they're liable to run out of patience, and move on.

Conversely, they'll notice when you serve them well. Over the years, I've met more than a handful of IT professionals who were clearly very talented, and willing to work hard, but who never developed a strong battery of customer service skills, and whose businesses suffered as a result. Often, their situations could be improved just by doing a little bit more to listen to their clients' concerns and show that they care. It doesn't take a lot of effort to treat people with sympathy and respect, but when customers start writing reviews online, your rapport is one of the first things they mention.

If a customer leaves, I approach the situation with

SMALL TOWN BOY, BIG CITY BUSINESS

humility and an open mind. No team is perfect, and, if there are kinks in our armor at Elevated Technologies, I want everyone I work with to feel comfortable speaking up. To foster this kind of environment, I regularly hold meetings where we talk about missteps and lessons learned, and it's always been an edifying experience. Folks are generally grateful for criticism, accepting it as a blessing rather than an insult, and the company has improved immensely as a result.

From a small town in Mississippi, I'd somehow made my way to the fourth largest city in the country. And, just eight years after seeing my boss at Spring Medical on stage in a downtown hotel, I was at the Houston Business Journal's Fast 100 ceremony, accepting my own plaque, surrounded by my newfound peers. Standing in the convention room, in front of hundreds of people, I thought back to the early days living  in Houston, when I knew literally no one in town, and when it had been a thrill just to see revenues pass a thousand dollars per day. After about a decade of paying our dues, revenues were climbing well above a million dollars per year, a milestone that everyone wants to reach.

SMALL TOWN BOY, BIG CITY BUSINESS

In 2016, Elevated Technologies turned ten years old. In recognition of my work as an entrepreneur, I was accepted into the "40 Under 40" Class of 2016. This prestigious award is given to the top 40 executives in the city under the age of 40. The company also appeared for a second year in a row on the list of Top 501 Managed Service Providers, a list of the top IT companies around the globe, by Channel Futures, a media group that covers the information technology industry. A recognition that Elevated Technologies continues to be awarded to this day. All these accolades gave me a chance to reflect on how the organization had matured and to appreciate my own unique journey.

I knew we were hardly on a downward trajectory, but I started to wonder if we were hitting another ceiling. After talking about it with a business coach and management consultant, who I was meeting with once a month, I considered relinquishing control of regular operations so that I would have more time to make big-picture plans. In view of the excellent work that Austin had already done as my right-hand man, I decided to promote him to chief executive officer on a trial basis. He fit into the role perfectly, and I've since made the position permanent.

SMALL TOWN BOY, BIG CITY BUSINESS

The change in leadership allowed me to look into other projects. One of my newer interests has been cyber security, and so I used some of my extra time to earn multiple certifications in the field, as well as a master's degree in Information Assurance and Cyber Security from Capella University; since then, I've actually taken the first steps to begin work on a doctorate. In addition to my academic pursuits, I also felt confident about putting my weight behind Triad InfoSec, a new venture to help keep information systems in the business community safe.

When times were tough, personally or professionally, I turned to close family members like my mom, or to military friends like Gary Moore, who I'd known since my days in Corpus. Besides being a fellow veteran and small business owner, he'd also gone through a divorce, which made him a relatable person to talk to when I went through a similar experience. Like me, Gary had struggled at times to find an appropriate balance between

SMALL TOWN BOY, BIG CITY BUSINESS

work and family, and he knew the level of sacrifice involved in getting a startup off the ground. I benefited from his wisdom, especially when we combined his knowledge of insurance, and my own technical expertise, to join forces to found another new venture, Cyber Security Insurance Group.

Later on, I had the privilege of doing some pro bono work for my fellow veterans. In the summer of 2017, shortly after Hurricane Harvey put cities on the Gulf under several feet of water, I started talking to someone from a non-profit based in Houston called Grace After Fire, which helps women access career resources and financial assistance after their time in the military. One of their clients had lost her home computer in the flooding, they explained. Libraries were her only other option, but these could be hard to get to, or were only available for a few hours a day, and, without better access, she was in danger of losing her job. I visited their office, and looked through some of the hardware components they had to possibly replace her machine. There wasn't really anything usable, so I decided to simply buy a new laptop and offer it as a gift. This kind of extracurricular work is very fulfilling, and I was thrilled for the chance to give back to my community. In 2019, Grace After Fire invited me to join their board of directors, and I've continued working to make their communications systems more efficient, while helping more veterans in the process.

SMALL TOWN BOY, BIG CITY BUSINESS

As Elevated Technologies has continued to grow, my priorities have opened up. A year ago, I decided to gather everything I'd learned on cybersecurity into a book. Small Business - A Hacker's Playground, was aimed at small businesses like myself. It was something of an unexpected project, since I was far from an English buff in high school, despite the protestations of my mom, an avid reader and published writer. But, when the book came out in print, she was as thrilled as anyone, and congratulated me on finally coming over to her side.

Not too long ago, my first company passed two million dollars in revenue. I'm feeling more motivated than ever, and, as my focus has shifted towards forming strategic, long-term partnerships for my companies, I've taken a step away from the day-to-day needs of the business. While I'm no longer the person executing things, I'm still a busy man, navigating my ship to keep the three companies growing, and keeping our clients happy. I know that there will be all sorts of setbacks and frustrations in my path—in fact, this is one of the only things that's guaranteed. But just like that nineteen-year-old kid in Bahrain, I know that I'll be able to handle it.

StoryTerrace

www.ingramcontent.com/pod-product-compliance
Lightning Source LLC
Chambersburg PA
CBHW040235220526
45473CB00001B/256